An Imaginary Menagerie

ROGER McGOUGH

Illustrated by Tony Blundell

PUFFIN BOOKS

For Matthew Joseph

PUFFIN BOOKS

Published by the Penguin Group
27 Wrights Lane, London W8 5TZ, England
Viking Penguin Inc., 40 West 23rd Street, New York, New York 10010, USA
Penguin Books Australia Ltd, Ringwood, Victoria, Australia
Penguin Books Canada Ltd, 2801 John Street, Markham, Ontario, Canada L3R 1B4
Penguin Books (NZ) Ltd, 182–190 Wairau Road, Auckland 10, New Zealand

Penguin Books Ltd, Registered Offices: Harmondsworth, Middlesex, England

First published by Viking Kestrel 1988
Published in Puffin Books 1990
1 3 5 7 9 10 8 6 4 2

Text copyright © Roger McGough, 1988
Illustrations copyright © Tony Blundell, 1988
All rights reserved

Made and printed in Great Britain by
Cox & Wyman Ltd, Reading
Filmset in Baskerville (Linotron 202)

PUFFIN BOOKS

AN IMAGINARY MENAGERIE

A teapet
I can recommend
to those who need
a loyal friend

And there are any number of other friends to choose from
in the strange world of the Imaginary Menagerie, where a
doodling squirrel rubs tails with a skating skink and the
allivator is more dangerous than he seems. Even with the
most ordinary of animals the unexpected is bound to
happen, so if you've never seen a budgerigar smoke a cigar
or a flamingo dance, be prepared for a few surprises.

An Imaginary Menagerie is a highly original collection of
animal poems with a difference from one of today's most
popular poets. Tony Blundell's witty illustrations
perfectly capture the extraordinary qualities of Roger
McGough's imagination.

Roger McGough was born in Liverpool, and in the late
sixties and early seventies he was a member of The
Scaffold. He is best known as a writer of plays and poems
for both adults and children, and he spends much of his
time performing his work on tour. He now lives in
London.

Contents

Ever heard
an aardvark
bark?

Miaows and birdcalls
all mill to its grist

South Africa's leading
veldtriloquist.

at the top.

then eat you

his back

ride upon

let you

he will

in a shop

see one

if you

allivator

Beware the

Ever see
an anaconda
drive through town
on a brand new Honda?

Don't ask him
for a ride

You might end up
inside.

Anglefish
are literally
trilateral

Living
quite littorally
comes natural

If you see one
near the reef
say hello

But what big teeth!
Is that a shark
down below?

Isosceles
are prone
to freeze

Growing colder
by degrees

In the dense
Euclidean seas.

Once upon a time,
there lived in the forest
Badgers and Goodgers

Badgers emerged only after dark
using foul language,
and gobbled up all the blind dormice,
deaf bats and lame frogs
they could lay their greasy claws on,
as well as choice morsels of any child
who happened to wander innocently
into the forest, way past its bedtime.

Goodgers, on the other hand,
were bright-eyed and light as marshmallows.
They loved to dance in the sunshine
and could sing in many languages.
When not jogging or clearing litter
they nibbled moon beans and alfresco sprouts
and ate lots of fibre.

And then suddenly, without warning,
there came The Great Drought
followed by The Great Fire
followed by The Great Flood
followed by The Great Plague
followed by The Great Jazz Revival

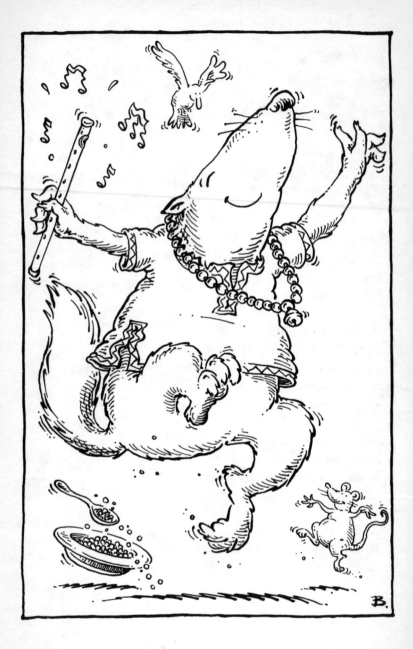

And when finally The Great Famine
took the forest by the throat

It was the Badgers
who wheeled and dealed
and looted and hoarded.
Who connived, ducked and dived.

And it was the Goodgers
who cared and shared
and helped those
less fortunate than themselves.

Unfortunately,
the less fortunate survived
and the Goodgers perished.
Which just goes to show.

And so when Pan
(The Great Spirit of the Animal Kingdom)
returned to the forest after a fortnight in Portugal
he was saddened by the demise of the Goodgers
and determined that they should not be forgotten.

So, dipping a finger
into the pure white pool of Goodger memory,
he annointed the heads of the Badgers
who immediately gave up swearing and eating children.

And to this very day,
Badgers still wear the distinctive white mark
on their coats   (As far as I know.)

Ever see
a beaver
wiv a cleaver?

(Nor me, neaver.)

What's that ticking
you hear in the closet?

It's the stopwatch beetle
that does it

It's timing
the dry rotting

In the old
wainscoting

And admiring
the eerie deposit.

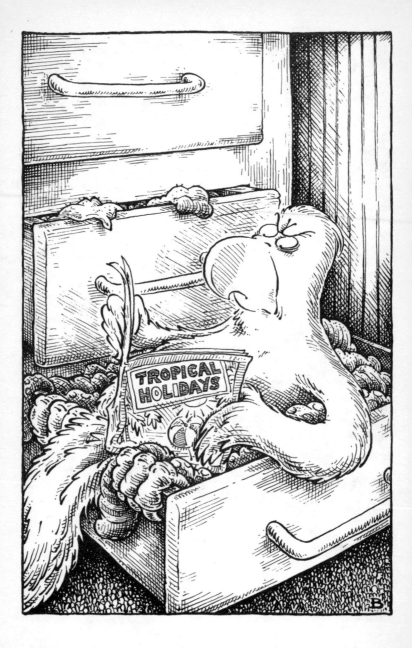

I used to keep
   a blue macaw
in my bedside
   bottom drawer

But he was never
   happy there
among my socks
   and underwear

He pined for sunshine
   trees galore
as in Brazil
   and Ecuador

Knowing then
   what I must do
I journeyed south
   as far as Kew

In the Gardens
   set him free
(wasn't that macaw-
   ful of me?)

Bookworms
    are the cleverest
of all the worms I know

While others
    meet their fate
on a fisherman's hook as bait

Or churn out silk
    or chew up earth
or simply burn and glow

They loll
    about in libraries
eating words to make them grow

(Vegetarians mainly,
    they are careful
what they eat

Avoiding names
    of animals
or references to meat)

They live
   to ripe old ages
and when it's time to wend

They slip
   between the pages
curl up, and eat 'The End'.

The Brushbaby
lives under the stairs
on a diet of dust
and old dog hairs

In darkness, dreading
the daily chores
of scrubbing steps
and kitchen floors

Dreaming of beauty
parlours and stardom
doomed to a life
of petty chardom.

Budgerigars
who smoke cigars

In the back
of large Rolls-Royces

Are mere poseurs
who put on airs

And seldom
have fine voices.

The Sopwith camel
is worth a mention
as an economic
fuel-saving invention

Pump the hump
with gasoline, and lo!

It flies across the desert
in one go.

Beware
the canary
gone hairy

Fed on steroids
instead of seeds

On humans now
this mutant feeds

A tweet like thunder
eyes that rage

Do not loiter
near its cage

Beware and be wary
There's nothing as scary
as a furry canary.

A catapillow
is a useful pet

To keep
upon your bed

Each night you simply
fluff him up

Then rest
your weary head.

Ever see
a chimp
with a limp?

That's because
they keep to trees

Twisted ankles
and scraped knees

In Monkeydom
are rarities.

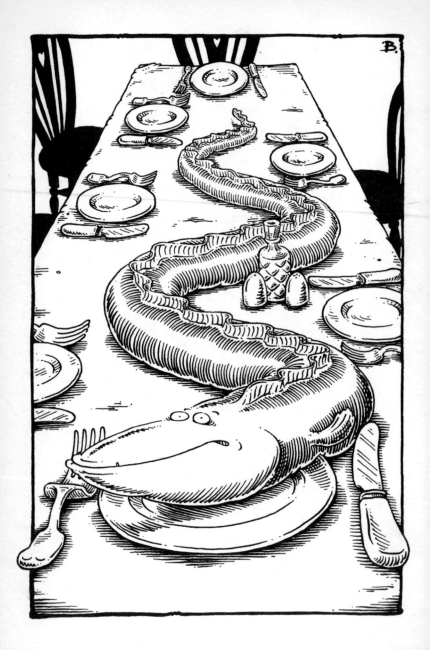

Is there
a longer meal
than a
conger eel?

Ever see
a dachshund
dash under
lavatory doors?

Like a
limbo-dancer
(caught short)
on all fours.

Ever see
a dik-dik
being sick-sick?

That's because
they hic-hic
when eating leaves
too quick-quick

This antelope's
bad table manners
are the talk
of the savannas.

Ever heard
a dingo
sing? O
you should

A Thing
in darkness
gargling
blood.

The doormouse
   is seldom seen
except perhaps
   at Halloween

The practical joker
   of his genus
to grown-ups he's
   a proper menace

The silly game
   he likes to play
is banging on doors
   then running away.

The durianimal
    is an amazing beast
(the word is Malaysian
    for 'unusual feast')

Low in calories
    and good to eat
an odd combination
    half-fruit, half-meat

In taste and texture
    beyond belief
imagine pineapple
    and rare roast beef

(To vegetarians
    they remain a puzzle
some refrain
    while others guzzle)

Growing on trees
    until mature
they drop from the branches
    and crawl on the floor

With yellowish leaves
     two legs and two arms
they live in the shade
     of the durian palms

But not for long . . .

Considered such
     a gourmet treat
their lives (like their bodies)
     are short and sweet.

Ever see
elephants
with
smelly pants?

The answer:
potty-training
during
elephancy.

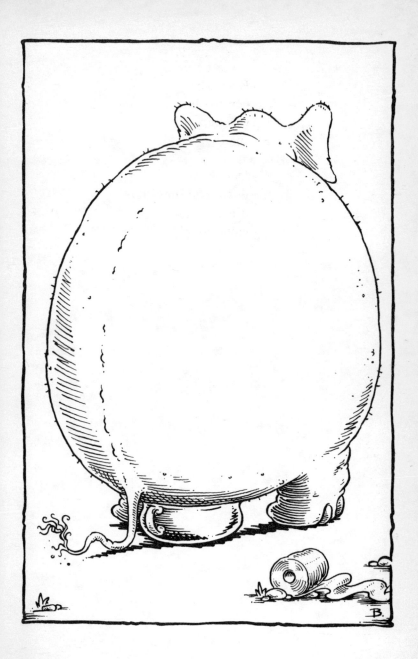

To amuse
    emus
on warm summer nights

    Kiwis
do wiwis
from spectacular heights.

How do
animals
procreate?

Faunacate.

Ever see
a flamingo
dance?

Passion
and romance
is what they adore

In the flash
of an eye
they take to the floor

Castanets
they click
with a flick of their bills

Then
paso doble
till pink in the gills

Flamingoes rule. Olé!

Ever see
a baby gibbon
with a bib on?

Primates are prim
and surprisingly neat
when eating breakfast
with their feet.

Duffle Goats
cling to mountainsides
at heights
that make one boggle

And are hunted
by old beatniks
in search
of a long-lost toggle.

Will a
gorilla
kill a
chinchilla?

No, because
they wouldn't dare
risk damaging
the fur of the rare
and expensive
coats they wear.

Ever see
a grass hopper
in a
crashed chopper?

As pilots go
they are
far too skilled
to fly too low
and risk being killed.

Starlings
are brave things
and grey ones
the most

Like the
Grey Starling
rescuing sailors
off the
Northumbrian coast.

Ever see
haddock
rock 'n' roll?

Mad on
reggae
blues 'n' soul

See them
shuffle
in a
soft-shoe shoal.

Hamsters
built the dams
on the banks
of the Zuyder Zee

Beside which,
on Bank Hollandaise,
the whole dam nation
likes to be

Dads and their old dutches
(even kiddies in their prams)
give three hearty cheers
for the good old hamsterdams.

Handfish
are grand fish

they swim
about in pairs

hold each other
when they fall in love

and when
they say their prayers.

*   *   *

They tickle
the sea's bare bottom

playful
as little kittens

and when
there's a nip in the ocean

wear brightly
coloured mittens.

Old hippos
   one supposes
have terrible
   colds in the noses

Attracted to these
   nasal saunas
germs build their nests
   in darkest corners

Then hang a sign
   that says politely
(streaming, streaming,
   day and nightly)

'Thank you for havin' us
in your nostrils so cavernous.'

Never
rely on
a lion

To repay
the debt
that he owes

Androcles
was a
liar

As the lion
that ate him
well knows.

Ever see
a llama
harm a
fly?

Not their
Kharma
that's why.

Ever see
a lobster
dine with
a mobster?

The Crayfish
Twins did

(and Abalone
knew Al Capone).

The Loch Ness Monster
Has just been spied
By a fisherman
Who almost died.

A dreadful thing, all scales and teeth
With sort of hairy bits beneath
(And that's only the fisherman!)

It lurks (the monster, i.e.)
In unfashionable depths under the sea
Swimming in and out of the loch
Through a tunnel cut deep in the rock.

A dozen sharks it eats for snacks
Octopie it loves to chew
Killer whales it breaks their backs
Is it true? Is it true?

Scottish folk don't easily scare
But most of them stay up in town
And only the very bravest dare
Sail alone when the sun goes down.

It swallowed an oil-rig in one gulp
Attacked a tanker and gobbled the crew
Battered a battleship into pulp
Is it true? Is it true?

I have a theory, and I'll put it to you . . .

Any Scot worth his salt likes a wee dram of malt.
Out there fishing, it's getting late
No one to talk to, only the bait
Nothing to do, but drink and wait
And drink and drink, and drink and . . . *wait!*

Out of the mist like an Angel of Death
Comes howling a monster with brimstone breath
Gigantic serpent, satanic messiah,
The stench of an abattoir on fire.

Closer and closer upon the port bow
He tries to row but it's too late now
It rears above him jaws agape
Upturns the boat – a chance to escape?

Swimming madly like never before
He strikes out blindly and reaches the shore
Loses the boat but escapes with his life
(Well, that's the story he'd tell his wife).

Short-sighted hunters
choose moose

A target as large
as an orphanage wall

The quicker the trigger
the harder they fall

Short-sighted hunters
go home to their wives

Hang hats on the antlers
live short-sighted lives.

Ever hear
a newt
play the flute?

Practising underwater
the classics and pop

See the bubbles burst
into music at the top.

Ever spend
a night in jail
with
a nightingale?

When he sings
catch the notes
and string them together
squeeze through the bars
run hell for leather.

nits

are   the

pits

Birds are feathered prayers
Offered up each day

To the Falconer upstairs
Let osprey.

One morning
an ostrich
buried his head
in the sand
and fell asleep

On waking
he couldn't remember
where he'd buried it.

Ever see
an oyster
in a cloister?

Then how about
a monkfish?

Do you have any pet peeves?
I have a pet peeve, his name is Spot

Does he live on a strict diet?
Yes, he loves his bowl of stricts

Does he charge around the neighbourhood?
About 50p an hour

Is he housetrained?
He occasionally peeves on the carpet

Do you smack him?
On the spot

Out damned Spot!

Ever see
a perch
in church?

Every Sunday they pray
to keep the Big Bad
Fisherman at bay

Sad to say
that sometimes
when kneeling in a pew
in an uplifted state
the hook slips through
and they rise to the bait.

A pigeon's
religion's
its own affair

Does God
have feathers?
Is St Peter's Square?

Ever eaten
  poodle strudel?

It's sensational
  with cream

I once had
  chihuahua cheesecake

(Or was that
  another bad dream?)

A porcupine
    that lost its quills
ran away from home
    and took to the hills

All day long
    it cried as it crawled
'No one can love
    a creature so bald.'

But it was wrong.

A handsome kestrel
    dropped by to say
'I Love You! I Love You!'
    Then snatched it away.

Goodness gracious!
The pterodactyl
won't be back till
the next Cretaceous.

Why is
a quokka
cock-a-hoop?

Cos in Oz
there's no demand
for quokka soup.

Ever see
a rattlesnake
wound around
a birthday cake?

Then go to
Colorado
where full of
bravado

Cowpokes
from the panhandles
blow out
the candles.

Ever see
a scallop
gallop?

Then go
to the track
at Ocean Bay

Where there's
sea-horse-racing
every day.

Seagulls are eagles
with no head for heights

For soggy old crusts
they get into fights

Out-of-tune buskers
beggars and screechers

Seagulls are not
my favourite creatures.

Ever see
a sea-lion
make a bee-line
for a rose?

Than sneeze
with pollen
up its nose

It prefers
to freeze
on friendly floes.

Ever see
a shark
picnic
in the park?

If he offers
you a bun

run.

Ever see
a skink
on a
skating-rink?

Lizards
though
wizards
on dry brick walls
show a tendency
to upendency
resulting in falls.

A 15-amp slug
you are likely to find
in the garden under a rock

Be careful
how you pick it up

You might get
a nasty shock.

A sowester
will keep you dry
when storms
toss the ship
that you're steering

But its squeals
will make you
want to cry
and wish
you were hard of hearing.

Ever see
a hairy spider
hide inside
an airborne glider?

The pilot panics
on seeing what's in

As both of them
begin to spin.

Squiggles
love to draw
they are simply nuts about sketching

Doodling
in tree-top garrets
while squirrels do the fetching

Swapping
each little picture
for a pawful of food

(Although
charging extra
for Miss Nutkin in the nude.)

A teapet
I can recommend
to those who need
a loyal friend

Quiet, reliable
he'll never stray
content to sit
on his kitchen tray

Give him water
stroke his spout
say 'thank-you'
when the tea comes out.

Ever see
a terrapin
bowling?

The pride
of the alley
is Dead-eye
Sally

Another strike
hear the crowds cheer!

(A pity her run-up
takes over a year.)

Ever see
a unicorn
one misty moisty
golden dawn
forlorn
upon a garden lawn?

Oh yes.
Near the roccery I suppose
where the rocs live?

Beneath the tree
where the gryphons nest?

Beside the pool
where the mermaid
combs her hair?

Oh look!
Flying in over Sainsbury's
a squadron of dragons.

A war thog
is a mercenary beast

Who will show you
no mercy
until you're deceased

Armed to the teeth
with tusks
like scimitars

If you see one
give it
the widest perimeters.

A
water bison
is what
yer wash
yer face in.

Said the Water Boatman
　　To the Water Boatmaid
'Won't you marry me?
　　We'll leave this boring pond behind
And sail across the sea.'

　　Said the Water Boatmaid
To the Water Boatman
　　'Thanks, but I've no wish
To leave my natural habitat
　　And feed the deep-sea fish.'

So the Water Boatman
　　Set off next day
To cross the ocean wide
　　Some say he lives on a tropical isle
Others say he died.

　　Said the Water Boatmaid
'How good to be free
　　And frail and pretty and young.'
And she sang a wee song
　　As she drifted along.

And she didn't hear the snap
Of the dragonfly's tongue.

And she didn't hear the snap
Of the dragonfly's tongue.

Weasels
at ease
at easels

Sables
at tables
tattoo

Hens'll kill
for pencils

And a cock'll
doodle too.

Ever see
a wombat
dressed
for combat?

By and large
his camouflage
is perfect

Khaki
from his head
to his toes

(Except for the helmet
which is orange, and glows!)

Wordfish
are swordfish
in a state of undress

Criss-crossing
the ocean
in search of an *S*.

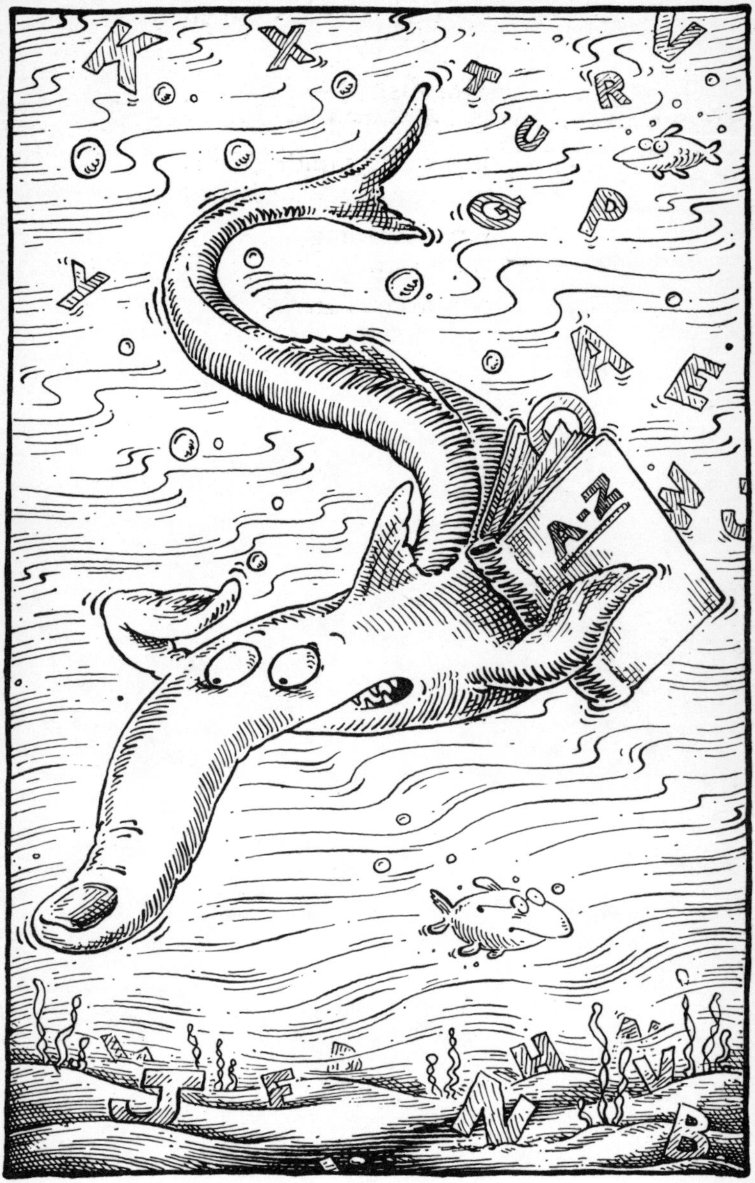
A-Z

Ever see
a yak
in a
yashmak
that shrunk

Ask for its
cash back
in a
casbah
full of junk?

A zonk
one must conclude
is good for nothing
and very rude

Preferring
plonk to food
it drinks all day
until it's stewed

Then passes out.
Zonk.

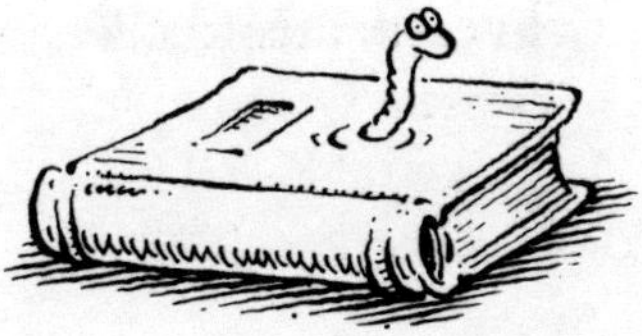

The Pattemitch
has a talent rich
and rare: it names
things. Gives titles.

Pattemitch, Pattemitch
Wordy Man
Make me a title
As fast as you can.

It gave me this to take away:
An Imaginary Menagerie.
Do I like it? Hard to say.

(For Brian Patten and Adrian Mitchell)

STARTLING VERSE FOR ALL THE FAMILY
Spike Milligan

The master of comic verse is back! Whether you're five or five hundred years old, you'll enjoy the irresistible poems that spill out of the pages of this new collection. A fun book for all the family and everyone else too.

CAT AMONG THE PIGEONS
Kit Wright

This is no ordinary collection of poems – there aren't many poetry books with singing potatoes, mad dinner ladies and zoobs in. What's a zoob? You'll have to read this book to find out!

SMILE PLEASE!
Tony Bradman

Neil has a problem with the wobbly wheel on his bike, then there's Helen who can't stop bouncing, and Sarah who can't stop skipping, and Paul who likes kicking his football against the wall . . . just a few of the great people we can meet in Tony Bradman's first collection of poetry, and there's plenty of fun on every page.

THE EARTHSICK ASTRONAUT

In this original and exciting collection of children's poems, chosen from entries to *The Observer* National Children's Poetry Competition, the earth is seen through many different eyes. Viewed from a distance by the astronaut and from the closest of quarters by the worm and the mole, our planet and its inhabitants show an infinite variety of shape and character, all drawn in vivid images by some of today's most promising young poets.

OF CATERPILLARS, CATS AND CATTLE
Poems about Animals
Chosen by Anne Harvey

Dogs and frogs, cats and bats, dragonflies and butterflies . . . all these creatures and more are to be found in the poems that make up this delightful anthology selected by Anne Harvey. Poems short and long, funny and sad, classic and modern; a very varied and enjoyable collection that will appeal to a wide range of readers.

POETRY JUMP-UP
Compiled by Grace Nichols

Dynamic, diverse, filled with life and music, this book brings together the voices of black writers from Britain, Africa, America, Asia and the Caribbean in an exhilarating contemporary anthology, compiled by one of today's top black British writers.

OUT AND ABOUT
Poems of the Outdoors
Chosen by Raymond Wilson

The great outdoors beckons in this poetry collection with promises of adventures, journeys into the unknown and games around the year, and strange and exotic people whose life is on the open road. With poems by Ted Hughes, Thomas Hardy, Stevie Smith, William Blake and Fleur Adcock, this is an inviting and entertaining anthology.

SOMETHING I REMEMBER
Poems by Eleanor Farjeon
Edited by Anne Harvey

Eleanor Farjeon captures all the vivid, familiar feelings and experiences of childhood from past and present. Special occasions such as Christmas, Hallowe'en, birthday parties and Pancake Day mingle with the more everyday events of breakfast and bedtime and bonfires in what is both a delightful and unforgettable collection of poetry for younger children.

THE JUNGLE CUP FINAL & OTHER POEMS
Richard Digance

In this original and humorous collection you can discover how cricket was introduced to civilization by the Snails and Tortoises, why icebergs are painted white, and why the Ants bother to enter the Jungle Olympics every year!